THE COMMON MUSHROOM

(*Agaricus campestris*).

MUSHROOM CULTURE

FOR

AMATEURS:

WITH FULL DIRECTIONS FOR SUCCESSFUL GROWTH
IN HOUSES, SHEDS, CELLARS, AND POTS, ON
SHELVES, AND OUT OF DOORS.

By W. J. May.

ILLUSTRATED.

LONDON:
L. UPCOTT GILL, 170, STRAND, W.C.

CONTENTS.

MUSHROOM CULTURE FOR AMATEURS.

CHAPTER I.

INTRODUCTION.

THE culture of Mushrooms is a matter of some importance in most places where a staff of gardeners is kept, and even in small places it is expected that a supply shall be maintained throughout winter and early spring. Although the successful culture of this esculent fungus is as easy as that of any other crop grown for table to those who know how to carry it on, and have the necessary appliances at command, yet with those who are not so well off, failures will from time to time occur ; but there is this consolation, that an observant person will see what and where the cause of failure is, and modify his future treatment accordingly. Some amateurs have an idea that any cellar however wet, or any shed however hot and dry it may be, will be a perfect structure in which to grow mushrooms, but they cannot make a greater mistake, as certain conditions must be fulfilled ere anything like success is attained.

Mushrooms do best in a moderately light, fairly ventilated place, free from any excess of moisture and yet not too dry, and so situated that the hot sun does not convert the structure into a small drying oven during the middle of the day. Mushrooms no doubt do spring up in the most unexpected and apparently unsuitable places, but it will be noticed, if the surroundings are carefully examined, that the place is not so unsuitable as it may at first sight appear. The largest natural bed of mushrooms we have seen was in an old disused stable, where they issued from every crack and crevice of the floor, which was rather badly paved with Dutch clinkers, but then the position was suitable, as the walls were quite 18in. thick, composed of rough stone masonry, and a very thick thatched roof protected the floor from the heat of the sun. If we examine the case fully, we find that the mycelium or spawn had a cool and properly moist bed in which to spread, and a steady equable temperature was maintained, while the atmosphere was moist, without being saturated with moisture. We came across the bed at the latter end of August, or early in September, so far as we can now remember, consequently such a place would have a regular temperature of about 60deg. Fahr., windows and doors being kept closed. On another occasion we found some of the large flooring tiles in a shed displaced, and on taking them up to search for the cause of their displacement, found a bunch of mushrooms of all imaginable forms, and distorted most grotesquely by the pressure.

It is no unusual thing to find mushrooms by the sides of sandy or chalky country roads, and we once found about half-a-dozen in the St. John's Wood-road, near Lord's Cricket Ground. These were growing in the road itself, at the base of a kerbstone, the largest mushroom being nearly expanded, and about an inch in diameter. Of course, such instances do not occur very often, but anyone who keeps a sharp look-out, now and again will have a " find," one that is not very valuable perhaps, but which is none the less interesting. Practically speaking, we should far rather expect to find mushrooms on a down or high-lying pasture than on a road, but, like insects, one often finds them where least expected.

Admitting the possibility of sometimes finding plants in apparently unsuitable places, and of accidentally getting a crop of any esculent in such positions, yet chance successes do not promise continual good luck to the persons who are thus able to score a novelty; and practically we prefer to grow plants in suitable situations. We have had mushrooms in dozens of unlikely places where heaps of loam, manure, &c., have been placed for other purposes, while on the other hand we have had more failures in such places when beds have been made purposely, and these have occurred in the majority of instances because the suitable conditions could not be artificially made. We admit that to have mushrooms on a house top, in a wine cellar, or in a kitchen cupboard, is something of which anyone can boast, and make matter for the newspapers, but at the same time where one person is successful a dozen would experience decided failures, and that simply because the position and the conditions of growth are of the most artificial and unnatural kind. We therefore counsel all intending cultivators to have the best conveniences for their purpose they can command, and also to follow in well beaten and successful tracks, rather than to mark out a new departure for themselves, as to which they are only confident that it *might* prove successful.

CHAPTER II.

NECESSARY CONDITIONS.

LIGHT, air, warmth, and moisture are as desirable for the successful culture of mushrooms as for other plants, and, where these cannot be commanded, only partial successes will be gained. It is true that mushrooms can be produced in the dark, and in a close atmosphere, but then, what are they like? They are thin-fleshed, pale coloured, and almost flavourless, useless for all purposes to which a mushroom is generally applied. A good mushroom should have a thick flesh, shape

FIG. 1.—FORCED OR BUTTON MUSHROOM.

like that shown in the frontispiece, be of a more or less brown colour, as cultivation makes some slight differences in this point, rich salmon-coloured gills, and, above all, a good flavour.

At Fig. 1 we give a very good illustration of the forced or button form of mushroom, such as is so largely grown in the caves near Paris for home consumption and exportation.

We, for our part, prefer a flat-roofed shed, facing the north, with windows, and means of ventilating, and then we reckon on a good crop of the best produce. The reason for having a shed with a flat roof is to equalise the heat as much as possible, and, were we building a mushroom house, it would be as in the illustration, Fig. 2, which shows a section of a house calculated to maintain the necessary atmospheric conditions for the growth of the crop intended. The house would be 12ft. wide, 8ft. high to the eaves, and with a span roof, flat-ceiled inside. We should prefer board walls filled in with cocoa fibre or sawdust, and a thatched roof, small windows

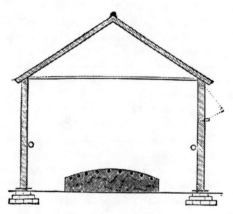

Fig. 2.—Section of Mushroom House.

for ventilation being placed alternately on either side the house. Such a structure would keep a regular temperature, and not be liable to the fluctuations of the weather, and one row of 4in. hot-water pipes, about 4ft. from the floor, would keep up the necessary heat in cold weather It is not, however, possible in all cases to have what one desires, and, in the majority of instances, a house that already exists has to be used for the purpose, and frequently even this is not to be had, and a stable, cellar, or other place must be utilised for mushroom culture. It is absolutely necessary that whatever structure is used for the purpose should be secure from wet, free from the influence of climatic changes, and capable of being maintained at a temperature of about 65deg. Fahr. Of course, ventilation is necessary, and light is desirable, but if this latter cannot be had we must put up with the somewhat lower quality of the crop. It is useless to attempt mushroom culture in cellars which are reeking with moisture, containing air foul enough to make a candle burn with a blue flame, or in a shed where everything is dried up on the first fine day, for in neither of these places could success be attained. Far better to have the beds out of doors, for then if the weather is at all favourable there is a chance of success which does not exist in unsuitable places. Mushrooms which come spontaneously in the open air, as a rule come most plentifully in fine autumns, after showers have quickened the mycelium or spawn into active growth. The soil is then moist and warm, and the air, although moist, is not surcharged with moisture, while the sun exerts a steady influence for several hours in the day.

To put the matter shortly, mushrooms do best when the soil, air, and weather are moist and warm ; and therefore to attain success in artificial culture these conditions should be imitated as nearly as possible by having a gentle warmth in the bed, a gentle atmospheric warmth (either natural or artificial), and a proper amount of moisture, both atmospheric and in the bed. Of course, the heat of the structure must be kept as uniform as possible, but this is a matter of practice.

There is one thing which is most essential to success, and that is good spawn, a part of the system of mushroom culture that must on no account be overlooked. It is useless to have old stuff that has no vitality, and, as a rule, this is what you get from the corn-chandler's or other small local seedshop. It does not pay these people to throw away or destroy their waste or unsold goods, and the result is that purchasers pay a high price for what is of little or no value. Always deal with a good firm, such as Sutton's, Carter's, Daniel's, &c., and then you will be certain of getting what you pay for. As a rule, we prefer what is termed milltrack spawn, but some of the commoner kinds give a good return at times. Of this matter, however, we will speak farther on.

CHAPTER III.

MATERIALS REQUIRED.

First and foremost in the culture of mushrooms comes the selection of proper materials for the formation of the beds, for although it may be fitting, and is indeed desirable, to have a proper house for the growth of this esculent fungus, yet such house would be of no manner of use if proper materials were not provided for the fungi to grow in. We say, therefore, that it is better to have good materials and grow an outdoor crop, than to have a building erected at great expense, and then stint the cost of materials by a few shillings and lose all the crop. We have never found it pay to stint any crop in this essential part of the process, for if we have loam we want the best and most suited to our requirements, and the same with peat, sand, manure, &c.; whatever you have, have the best; but you need not pay fancy prices nevertheless. It is idle to use things which are not suited to the purpose for which they are intended; and, if purchased because they are low in price, they will be found quite the reverse of cheap. In mushroom culture three articles only are required—horse manure (generally called "droppings"), cow manure, and loam, and of these the cow manure is often most conspicuous by its absence.

The best kind of horse manure is, without doubt, that which is collected in a dry state on a sandy road, as such is less liable to rot than that from a stable. Rottenness and decay are adverse to the growth of mushrooms, and, therefore, the greatest care should be exercised in getting things for manure in a fresh and sweet state. When manure which has been collected from

roads cannot be had, then fresh stable dung as free from straw
as possible, should be obtained, and on no account should it be
mixed with cinders or other rubbish, as the object should be to have
a clean and sweet fermenting material, free from all foreign admix-
tures. Rotten manure is useless for all practical purposes, and
should never be used.

Cow manure is best when collected in a half-dried state from a
meadow, as it is then free from straw and rubbish, besides being
free from superfluous moisture. The great fault in this manure,
when obtained from sheds, is the vast amount of moisture which it
contains, and also that the variety of food which is given to stall-fed
animals causes the quality to be anything but regular. We therefore consider, when cow manure is used, that it should be collected from the fields where cattle are turned out to graze. It
should be in a partially dried state, so that the excess of water
is eliminated, and, when collected, should be thrown up in a heap,
and not trodden on.

Loam should be of a somewhat stiff nature, yellow loam, or that
from the London clay—yclept, in nursery parlance, "maiden loam."
It should be the top 4in. or 5in. dug off with the turf on it;
but it should be closely fed or mown before digging, so as to be
free of an excess of grass and other green herbage, and it should
be moist but not saturated when dug. It is well to avoid soils
containing rusty-looking streaks, and also that which is liable to
be flooded at times, because thereon mushrooms will be rarely
found. Where loam of a stiff nature is not to be had, of course
the best substitute must be taken, and that is perhaps the top
2in. or 3in. from a calcareous common or down, as on such,
mushrooms generally grow with great prolificacy, and therefore it
is to be chosen before a sandy loam, which, in its turn, is better
than soil highly charged with humus or decayed vegetable matter.

In fact, mushrooms, as a rule, abhor rotten or partially rotten
vegetable substances of any kind; therefore the greatest care
should be taken to keep clear of such things.

CHAPTER IV.

PREPARATION OF MATERIALS.

As we mentioned before, decomposed materials are of no use for the work in hand, nor is it at all desirable that rapid decomposition should set in after the beds are made, as such would defeat the end in view; therefore a careful preparation of the materials is needed. If the horse droppings are collected from a road in dry weather, and placed in a heap, as collected, they will generally be fitted for use as soon as a sufficient quantity is got together; but if, after they are collected, they be passed through a sieve of 1in. mesh, they will be much improved, as they will then be more regularly incorporated. In fact, where time can be spared for the purpose, it is always the better plan to sift the droppings, as by this means they are rendered pretty equal in all points, and there is not that tendency to over-heat which is present in roughly-made beds. Beds which over-heat either get dry and lose their heat and value, or they decay and so become useless. Anyone who cares to take the trouble to go where mushrooms are largely grown will find that the manure used for the beds, when they are exhausted, is not very greatly altered in appearance, it is not rotten, and it has a smell quite different to the fresh material. To this may also be added that it has lost nearly all the nitrogenous matters it orginally contained, and is of small use as a stimulating manure, although it does well for early potatoes or other crops that do not require a rich, fat manure. If too dry, water should be added through a fine-rosed water-can, the mass being mixed and turned from time to time till an uniform state of moisture is obtained. When uniformly moist throughout, and in a state which is calculated to retain its heat and moisture for a length of time, the material is fit for use, and should be treated as described further on.

On the other hand, and distinct from the above directions, which are fit and just for fine weather, we have to consider the preparation of materials in wet and sloppy weather, and this opens up quite a different mode of preparation. Instead of having to damp the materials down, we shall have to dry them, and that without fermentation or causing decomposition to set in, so that actually much care must be exercised in preparing the materials. In the first place, about the right quantity of droppings must be got together, and for a small bed about a cart load, or what is its equivalent, ten ordinary box barrow loads, and these should be laid thinly over the floor of an open shed. Each day the material should be turned over and well shaken, and when it has laid a week or more, according to the amount of moisture it contains, the whole should be thrown up into ridges of moderate size, and these should be thrown over lightly on alternate days until the whole is fit for use. We have ere now had to work the material for a month before it has been dry enough to use. There is, however, a very great deal of gain in thoroughly preparing the materials in the first place, as such preparation tends to increase both the duration and fertility of a bed. Where a good knowledge of the subject is not possessed by the cultivator, a little hurry, or the use of too wet material, frequently causes loss of the largest part of the crop; perhaps not above a week has been gained in the preparation of the beds, while from six weeks to two months, or more, is lost by the failure.

Persons who have not the patience to wait for the materials to be got in good and proper order for the mushrooms to do well should only grow mushrooms when the materials need no preparation. To grow mushrooms well needs a certain amount of care in the preparation of the materials, and if this cannot be afforded, why, of course, failure will be sure to result, either wholly or in part. When the material — *i.e.*, the horse manure—is in a proper state so far as moisture is concerned, the whole should be thrown up in a heap to get warm, and it is at this stage that about a tenth part of loam or nearly dry cow manure can be well mixed with it, as that tends to keep the beds somewhat longer in bearing when they are in a proper house, and, besides, gives the mushrooms generally a much thicker and firmer flesh. Of course, we make no reference here to the soiling of the beds. Loams should be dug about six months before they are wanted, and should be thrown up in conical heaps about four feet high and the same in width till needed for use. They should then be chopped down fine, and all large stones taken out, but they do not need sifting. The object is to get a good sweet loam of good texture, free from growing plants or moisture. In fact, a loam in good condition for potting purposes is just right for mushrooms. Cow manure should be gathered and laid up in a heap, so that the air can get amongst it, and the heap kept in a shed, or some other place under cover. In using, the dryest portion should be taken for mixing with the bulk of the other manure, and the wettest portion for soiling the beds.

CHAPTER V.

MAKING BEDS UNDER COVER.

PREPARATORY to making a mushroom bed, it is necessary to see that the floor on which it is to be placed is free from all liability to become flooded, as a mistake in this respect may prove costly in wet weather. We have seen sheds and outhouses ere now where the floors have been below the paths outside, and where the door sills have been defective; then the floors have been flooded to a depth of several inches in heavy storms of rain. We have pointed out before that an excess of moisture is opposed to the production of good crops, and, therefore, care should be taken in the first place that an excess of moisture cannot possibly obtrude itself. Where the floor is too low, and it is intended to make a practice of growing mushrooms on it, it should, if possible, be raised to a proper height by means of a layer of chalk well rammed down, and dusted over with some well-sifted coal ashes. Where, however, chalk is not to be had, brick rubbish, broken sandstone, or other materials of a like nature can be used, and if rammed down tight and covered with fine ashes will make a good bottom, and will stand the wear of the wheel-barrow.

When assured that no flooding out will occur through the floor, it is desirable to see that the roof and sides are also waterproof, because, where a drip from the roof occurs, the bed is spoiled for a space of quite a foot in diameter. The walls must be practically sound, or sometimes the rain will beat through, and at other times cold blasts of wind will render all attempts to maintain a regular temperature futile; it therefore behoves us to be careful in these respects, especially when we go in for winter work, as much expense both in labour and money may be incurred, and failure result through inattention to structural defects which would only have cost a few shillings, or perhaps only a few hours' labour, to rectify. Where houses are heated by hot water, great care should be taken that everything is in sound going order, and that no fear of a breakdown exists, as such would, in the majority of cases, mean a failure.

Everything being in readiness and the materials in a proper state of preparation, the beds should be made. We prefer to have any mushroom bed in the middle of the shed or building as shown in Fig. 2, such permitting a uniform temperature being kept up, and also allowing plenty of room to gather the produce, whilst a barrow can be wheeled along if necessary; 2½ft. is quite wide enough for these alleys or paths, and supposing a shed is 12ft. wide, this will allow a bed 7ft. wide and as long as is convenient.

Having marked out this space for the bed, it should then be prepared as follows: On the space to be devoted to the bed, lay a moderate thickness of coarse, sweet litter, say to a depth of 3in. or 4in. On this layer of coarse stuff place the prepared material to a depth of about 2ft. or 2½ft., and it should then be firmed down with the feet, by treading over once. Great care should be taken that the materials are well mixed, and of an even nature throughout, as previously directed, or the result will be other than good, and whole or partial failure will result. After the bed has reached as high a temperature as it will attain, it should, on declining to a temperature of, say 145deg., or if it is necessary to get the bed on as soon as possible, 150deg., be trodden and beaten firm; in fact, it should be rammed with a wooden rammer till no impression can be made in it, and until the whole of the materials are levelled down.

Great care must be taken that the sides of the bed are not beaten out, and that all is finished off in a workman-like manner; for although it may not make much difference in the quantity or quality of the crop, yet it is most awkward to have badly shaped beds. We prefer having a board along each side of the beds, as by this plan they are kept in shape better than without, for persons are apt to kick the sides of the beds and so cause a large portion to become disarranged, and a consequent loss of productive surface; and besides, a broken place allows of a too rapid loss of the heat contained inside.

When the heat has declined to a mean temperature of from 80deg. to 90deg., holes should be made with a blunt dibble, arranged about 5in. or 6in. apart, and about 2in. deep; in these the spawn should be placed, as presently described. If, however, the heat of the bed seems inclined to get much above 90deg., it is well to leave spawning for a few days longer, as too high a temperature is sure to destroy the mycelium. When the bed is beaten over, and before the holes are made, the cakes of spawn should be placed in lukewarm water for about five minutes, and then laid on the surface of the bed till the time for placing in the bed arrives. When the heat is right and the holes are made, break the cakes of spawn into pieces the size of large eggs, and place one piece at the bottom of each hole, afterwards filling the hole with some broken horse droppings, pressing them in firmly, but being careful not to break the pieces of spawn, as such would tend to cause failure. We always lightly tread the beds over after spawning, as we consider such treatment tends to ensure a better and more level crop, and make all parts of the bed of an equal consistency.

After spawning, what is technically called " soiling " is necessary, and this process consists in adding a layer of soil to the surface of the bed. There is, however, some little divergence of opinion on this point so far as the exact time of applying the earth, for while some cultivators hold that the soil should be put on as soon as the bed is spawned, others say that an interval, varying from two days to a week, should elapse. Our practice, however, has taught us that it is of little importance whether there is an interval or not, so long as too long a time does not elapse before the soiling is done. The surface of the bed should not get dry ere the earth is applied, and that is about the chief point.

Soiling consists simply in placing a layer of loam in a fairly dry state, *i.e.*, free from wetness, over the beds, and the haste with which the crop is needed will decide the thickness, because if a crop is needed in about six weeks, an inch of soil is ample;

but if one can afford to wait for another fortnight, he can put on a couple of inches of soil, and will have then a heavier crop. Spread the soil equally over the bed and tread firm, and afterwards pat level with the back of a smooth spade.

Some growers put on about an inch of cow manure before they put on the loam, and claim that it causes the beds to keep lower in bearing, but we have not found such to be the case. When the loam or other soil is sandy or poor, we have, however, found an improvement in the *quality* of the crop. Where good loam is to be had, we do not think there is much advantage in the layer of cow manure, but where the loam is poor it is well to use it. (This layer is not shown in Fig. 3.)

After this the place can be cleaned up, and a temperature of about

FIG. 3.—MUSHROOM BED.

60deg. maintained in the house, the bottom heat of the bed being about 5deg. to 10deg. above that. The nearer, however, the beds keep to about 60deg., the better and more lasting will be the crop. In Fig. 3 we give a sketch of a finished bed, showing the various layers of materials, spawn, &c. We show a bed with boards at sides, as such is more easily managed by amateurs, for the reason before stated. The bottom heat should always be tested with a proper instrument, which consists in a long copper tube, with thermometer, &c., fitted for the purpose of testing bottom heat. The "test stick" process is unreliable, and should never be used.

CHAPTER VI.

TREATMENT OF BEDS UNDER COVER.

At present we are only treating of such beds as are used generally by the gardener and amateur for ordinary work, and for other forms of bed a somewhat different treatment will be needed. After the beds are spawned and soiled down, nothing is needed but to keep the house fairly dry and sweet, and to maintain a regular temperature. In dry, hot weather, however, the beds should be covered with mats and the paths kept damp, to cause a healthy and proper moisture in the air, without which no kind of vegetable growth will thrive. Mind, we do not advise the use of houses for mushrooms in hot weather, but it sometimes happens that such have to be used, and, therefore, one should be ready for emergencies. A certain amount of humidity is necessary, but it should not be excessive, enough to prevent absolute dryness being quite sufficent.

When the mushrooms begin to push forth above the soil, a gentle and slight sprinkling should be given through a very fine rosed watering-pot, and the water applied should be about 4deg. or 5deg. warmer than the temperature of the house. The object of this sprinkling is more to prevent the breaking up of the beds than to apply any quantity of moisture to the embryo mushrooms; and this breaking up and loosening of the soil is often very troublesome when a large amount of fire heat has to be applied to keep up the necessary temperature during periods of climatic inclemency. After this sprinkling, it is a good plan to lay mats over the beds to keep the necessary moisture and yet admit of ventilation.

Hay, straw, and other litter we dislike, for several reasons; in the first place, it is liable to break and destroy a large part of the crop; in the second place, it harbours slugs, wood-lice, and other objectionable pests; and thirdly, it is apt to get damp and mildewed, the result being that the mushrooms are rotted off ere they are of any size. Of course, we are not referring to outdoor beds here.

When the crop is fairly swelling, and above ground, a fair but not excessive soaking should be given, and this will at once start the crop into rapid growth. The mats may at this time be removed, unless the house or shed be a very dry one, in which case they can be retained; but care will have to be taken in lifting them on and off the beds, or the mushrooms will be knocked off or broken. Precautions must be taken that the beds are not steamed too much with these mats, because such treatment is quite as bad as having the surface of the beds too dry. Should the surface of the beds become sticky, the mats should be taken off at once, and only a gentle dewing be given at intervals. As a rule, all heated mushroom houses should have both beds and paths gently dewed over with tepid water from a fine-rosed syringe about twice or, if the weather is cold and much fire heat necessary, thrice a week with tepid water, and perhaps once in three weeks or a month a good soaking should be given with water several degrees warmer than the atmospheric temperature of the house.

The length of time a bed will remain in bearing is a matter governed by local influences, and consequently no time for the continuance of these waterings can be given without knowing the full particulars as to site, &c., and even then local knowledge is the best guide. Where the house will permit of its being done, always give plenty of light to mushrooms, and also a fair amount of ventilation where such can be allowed with safety, as it tends to cause a better class of crop. Where light and air are given, mushrooms have thick flesh, and are solid and heavy; but when grown in dark, unventilated cellars or other similar places, they are thin in the flesh and of poor flavour, particularly where the spawn is not

CHAPTER VII.

SELECTION OF SPAWN.

BEFORE describing what is a good cake of spawn, it will be necessary to give a slight history of its manufacture, and for our purpose, only the cake spawn need be described. As most persons know, mushroom spawn is sold in cakes, of which there are from ten to fifteen or sixteen in the bushel, and the price ranges from 3s. to 5s. 6d. per bushel; as a general rule, the higher-priced is the cheapest, as it is generally fresh and well preserved. As we have before pointed out, spawn that has been wetted, or kept in a damp place, soon deteriorates, and then spoils; therefore it is very desirable to have that which is actually the best. Spawn keeps best in a dark place which is not too much ventilated, but yet has some amount of ventilation, and where the temperature is about 50deg. Here the spawn or mycelium will retain its vitality from six months to almost as many years in exceptional cases, but in practice it should not be more than, if as much as six months old. We prefer it about a month old, as then there is, in our opinion, the greatest chance of success, for drying the cakes at this time—not making them dust dry however—makes the mycelium wake into active life at once.

The way spawn is prepared is somewhat as follows: A quantity of clean horse droppings, cow manure, loam, and gritty sweepings from a gravelled road are got together, and mixed in about the proportion of three loads horse droppings, one load each of loam, road sweepings, and cow manure, all free from straw and long litter of all kinds. These materials are thoroughly mixed together, and not allowed to ferment and heat too much, or they would spoil for the purpose in hand, and when in a proper state of preparation are moulded to the proper shape and size in moulds very like those used in brick-making, by pressing and beating. A depression is made in each cake for the reception of the piece of old spawn which is to leaven or inoculate the new cakes. The cakes are laid out on the ground to dry somewhat, and are afterwards stood on edge to dry sufficiently for pairing and inoculating, which is done by placing each two cakes flat together, with the depressions inside, and in these depressions placing a piece of old spawn cake that is full of living mycelium. The cakes are then stacked away in dry sheds, and covered with sweet fermenting material sufficiently to cause a heat of about 65deg., or perhaps 70deg., but not more, as from 63deg. to 67deg. Fahr. is the best for inducing rapid and successful growth of the mycelium. After the thread-like formation has spread from the pieces of old spawn through the whole of the mass of new cakes—and these latter are full of a network of mycelium—then the cakes are taken and set on edge in some place where they will dry rapidly and perfectly, after which they are stored away.

We have not written this brief description with the idea that persons who read it will start making their own spawn, because that would be an absurdity. Our idea is that with such a rough description as we have given, readers will be able to select the best of the cakes of mycelium which are offered for sale; and if they choose such as are full of the white threads of spawn, of even consistency in the make, and which have a sweet mushroomy smell, they will not be far wrong. On the other hand, if the cakes be full of dark patches, and the threads of mycelium be dark brown or black, having an offensive smell, the cakes are of little value, if any, and should not be taken. With "Mill-track" and French spawn the same remarks apply as to smell and freshness of the threads of mycelium; but as the material is in a different form, the other remarks do not apply.

———————— · :=◆ ◆=: · ————————

we give a sectional sketch of a lean-to house constructed of Lascelles'
patent concrete slabs, one of the best things we have yet found for
garden shedding, as it is fireproof, durable, and a good non-conductor of heat. Our sketch represents a house 7ft. wide and the
same height in front, and if desired in such a place, wide shelves
could be placed along the back wall, and on these seakale, lilac, or
other forced goods could be prepared, as light could be excluded
when necessary. Practically, the cultural directions are the same
for this class of work as for shed work, but, perhaps, the following
points must be more closely attended to. Of course, we suppose
that the materials are well mixed and prepared as previously
described, and that the same care is taken in making the bed, as
without this success can scarcely be expected.

As mushroom houses are heated—and we personally prefer that
the pipes should be from three to five feet above the ground—unless
some method of applying atmospheric moisture is adopted, the air
will be so dry as to parch the surface of the bed and any mushrooms
or other growth that may appear. Now the best plan to prevent
this excess of dryness is to keep the paths dewed over with clean
water from time to time so that a steady amount of moisture will be
evaporated, and also to sprinkle the beds now and again as before
described. The chief object in having the hot-water pipes a good
height from the beds is to secure an equal diffusion of heat without
having an excess close to the beds, which would cause undue dryness
in the materials of which they are composed. While giving this
proper amount of heat and moisture, it is at the same time very
necessary that an excess of either should be carefully avoided, or, as
we have pointed out, the results will be very unsatisfactory. In any
case where fire heat is used the beds will need watering more often
than in a place where such is not used, and it is therefore well to
have the house so constructed as to need as little artificial heat as
possible consistent with maintaining the proper temperature.

As a series of beds are necessary to maintain a succession of crops,
it is well to have the house of a good length (from 20ft. to 40ft., as
circumstances will permit), and then to make separate beds about

once in three weeks till the house is full, renewing each bed again as it becomes worn out, as, with the exception of July and August, mushrooms do well under cover all the year round. A house 30ft long will allow of five beds 6ft. in length being made, and these will keep up a supply to any ordinary-sized family, but with large establishments larger houses should be arranged.

It is a strange thing that, while mushrooms are always largely in demand, very few gardens have suitable accommodation for their cultivation. In many places where there are sheds or houses put aside for the purpose, they are often not of the best, and, while large sums are spent in the erection of structures for other purposes, no great attention is paid to that for the culture of mushrooms, although they are very profitable.

Garden mushrooms can rarely be bought retail for less than 1s. per lb., and frequently the price is as high as 2s. 6d. at ordinary times; but few persons grow for market, and these make a good price, from 6d. to 5s., according to demand and season, but, on an average, 8d. to 1s. 6d. may be taken as the range, and at this it pays well, because, with the exception of the spawn, the waste material fetches a good price, from 4s. 6d. to 6s. per cartload being given for the beds when they are exhausted for the production of mushrooms.

We are not here advising mushroom culture as a profitable trade investment, as it depends on many contingent circumstances as to whether profit can be made on it as a business, the supply of manure necessary for the work not at all times being forthcoming, and if one has to pay more than 6s. per ton for this, and also to pay a long price for loam as well, it considerably takes the gilt off the profits, and in many instances will cause the balance to be on the wrong side. In private places, however, where one or two carriage horses are kept, and the manure costs nothing, it pays to have a place for mushroom culture, as a useful crop is obtained without seriously deteriorating the manure for use on the flower borders, or for potatoes; in fact, we have found in many cases that these latter have less disease than where fresh manure is used.   Anyhow, we advise the erection of a mushroom house where no such place exists, and if it is built against a house facing the north, or in a place over-shaded with trees, what is at present an unprofitable part of the garden may be made to pay a fair interest.

CHAPTER IX.

CULTURE IN SHEDS.

By culture in sheds, we mean in such unheated buildings as are to be found in many places, and which are used generally as store-houses for various odds and ends of greater or less utility and value, which may, however, be only too often classed as useless. Many old barns, coach-houses, fowl-houses, and similar places, which are double-boarded or have thick walls, and ceiled or thatched roofs, and are therefore practically frost-proof, would serve the purpose excellently, as in these mushroom culture can be carried on very successfully ; and, as it is only a utilisation of what already exists in an unprofitable form, we have not to reckon any further cost on the building account than the necessary repairs, which, of course, depend on the present state of the building. Of course, to be at all profitably utilised, these places must be weather-proof, and, above all, the roofs must be sound and free from drip, or the beds will be wholly or partially spoiled.

Generally hard frosts seriously hinder a crop, and if the beds are getting near the end of their time of production they will not retain sufficient heat, even with the best of coverings. Where, however, they are new, by the aid of good coverings of some fair non-conductor of heat and cold, although the bearing power of the beds may be hindered for a time, they soon become profitably productive when the frost goes away and a rise of temperature occurs.

Unheated structures are best in autumn and spring, giving the best crops at those seasons, and, indeed, it is a matter of good policy not to try to have crops when hard frosts may be reasonably expected, unless the house in which they are grown is practically frost-proof, and also free from draughts of cold air, as these soon reduce the temperature of both atmosphere and bed to a very low point.

The form in which the bed is made is the same as previously described, and the same care and trouble in preparation is needed with the material; but after the bed is made and spawned, a somewhat different mode of treatment is necessary. The beds need less water as a rule, and fewer sprinklings will be necessary. The matter of sprinkling will depend on the season, and whether it is very dry inside the shed, as great variations exist in this. Of course, when the shed is dry and the atmosphere is also dry, a certain amount of moisture must be applied, as before pointed out; but no more than is necessary should be used, or the temperature will be seriously

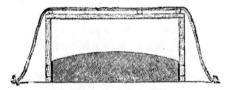

FIG. 5.—PLAN FOR PROTECTING BEDS FROM FROST.

reduced and a check given to the productive power of the bed or beds. In fact, it would be a wise plan to have a boiler and pipes fitted to all sheds of any size, so that artificial heat could at any time be applied when necessary.

As protection is necessary from fluctuations of temperature, we think it well to describe a form of covering we have used with marked success ere now. It is cheap, effective, and easily applied, and within the reach of everyone, and can generally be had without expense where a garden of any size is kept up. The first thing to be done is to make a frame at each end of the bed, as shown in Fig. 5, and on the top of this place ordinary garden stakes, about 1ft. or 18in. apart, as shown in the engraving. Over this framework ordinary mats are stretched, as shown, and pegged down, the mats being about 1ft. above the bed. In severe weather a good layer of dry litter, 1ft. or more in thickness, can be placed, or even warm litter from the manure heap can be used, which would help to keep up the right temperature. The space between the mats and the bed containing a quantity of air prevents the moisture from doing much harm, and as the mats are covered from the floor upwards, cold blasts of wind cannot enter. At the same time the mats at either end should be opened each day for a short time to allow of a certain amount of ventilation, and prevent the contained air becoming foul and stagnant.

By using a frame and mats as shown, the crop is not broken about or damaged, as would be the case if the litter was placed directly on the beds. We never like litter on the beds where it can be avoided, as it breaks the crop about as a rule, and as a rough frame and mats cost little, and give so much better results, it is really worth the making. Where precautions cannot be made in this or some other manner against frost, sheds should not be used except when there is no liability to frosts of a severe nature.

CHAPTER X.

CULTURE IN CELLARS.

MUSHROOMS can frequently be grown in cellars when they cannot be grown in the regular houses or outdoors, and particularly in the hot summer months, because, as a rule, underground buildings are generally not too hot for the purpose. Besides, cellars are generally of an equable temperature, and although, perhaps, very badly ventilated, no very great difficulty need exist in making them fit for the purpose we have in view. Of course, wet places where the water streams down the walls, and which are undrained, cannot be made into suitable houses for mushroom culture any more than they could be converted into ice-houses, for they would be too wet for either, and it is only such cellars as are well drained and in fairly dry situations that can be profitably utilised in growing these esculents.

Provided the place decided on is well drained and fairly dry, ventilation is the next point, and frequently a little trouble will be found in this respect. Of course, a door will exist, and if on one's own property, an entrance could be made for a 6in. drain pipe at the other end, as shown in Fig. 6. Holes should be made in the top of the door, and then the current of air will go in the direction shown by the arrows, thus exhausting the impure air at the bottom of the cellar. For more purposes than one, this system of ventilation is usually adopted, unless the cellar be under a public road, in which latter case, with a little ingenuity, ventilation can be applied at the back.

Having obtained the requisite ventilation, the bed should be made up in the manner before described; and here will be found the advantage of the method of ventilation described, for instead of having an atmosphere charged with ammoniacal gases, a sweet and healthy one will prevail. We have seen many attempts at mushroom culture in cellars where there has been no ventilation, and where the walls have been reeking with fetid moisture, and in such cases failure has been the result. On the other hand, we have seen as good results in dry well-ventilated cellars as could be obtained in the best houses. As a rule, but a small amount of watering is necessary, there being but a small amount of evaporation in cellars, and as there is generally a very equable temperature, but little artificial heat is needed in the coldest weather. It is, however, in the hottest

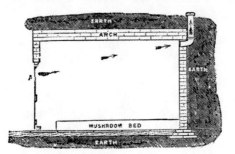

FIG. 6.—PLAN FOR VENTILATION OF CELLAR.

months of the year when cellar work is the most valuable, as then more certain results can be had.

It need hardly be said, we do not advise the erection of cellars for mushroom culture, as such would certainly be a great waste of capital with only a remote chance of profit, but where cellars already exist they can be utilised for the purpose, and frequently very profitably. As to the general rules of culture, they do not in any way essentially differ from that given before, but some amount of adaptation must at times come into play, for no positively hard and fast rules can be made, because in all kinds of cultivation the grower must use a certain amount of skill and forethought. There is really no royal road to success in gardening in any branch, and the traditionary ounce of practice is before any fixed rule. Cellars form a very useful adjunct to the regular mushroom house, and, in the absence of the latter, can be made to fulfil many of the purposes for which it is used, but still they are not necessities in mushroom culture in any form.

CHAPTER XI.

CULTURE IN POTS.

WE are now going to speak of a way of growing mushrooms which to many will perhaps sound as chimerical as it did to us, until we had a little success in the matter. Mushrooms in pots—unless they be placed there entire—certainly sounds absurd, but as a positive fact they can be so grown. One point, however, will remain an obstacle at all times to this plan, and that is the fact that it is not a profitable business; indeed, for aught but a curiosity of cultural skill, the whole process is a waste of time and trouble, but still a good pot of mushrooms is not a bad "show." Our readers must not suppose that we are enamoured with the idea, or that we propose they shall convert their cupboards into mushroom houses to the exclusion of their more legitimate use; but as most gardeners, both amateur and professional, have some pride in giving surprises both to friends and employers, of course this has a little novelty in that direction. At the same time the idea is not new; in fact, it was pointed out some forty years back, and we only adopted the plan to suit our own fancy.

To succeed in this method of culture it is desirable to have a place where the heat is about 65deg. to 70deg., and where a certain amount of atmospheric moisture exists, so that no watering of the pots occurs unless really necessary. Our pots have been best managed in a house at about 68deg., where a bench and cocoa fibre for plunging kept the pots in an uniform state of warmth and moisture. Of course, the glass roof was kept shaded with mats to exclude sunlight, and inverted pots were placed over those containing the spawn. The way we set about the matter was to fill

some pots two-thirds full of the finer portions of loam and manure
used in making a bed, and this material was compressed into them
very firmly.   The pots were then plunged in the fibre, and when at
about 70deg. pieces of spawn were placed in them, and they were
then filled firmly with good loam.   In from six weeks to two months
mushrooms were more or less freely produced, and were rather
curiosities ; but unless one has the time and space to spare, it is not

FIG. 7.—SECTION OF POT, SHOWING POSITION OF SPAWN, &c.

worth while to go in for pot work.   At the same time, a few pots
can be done with little trouble where a structure exists for the
culture of mushrooms, and sometimes they can be grown under the
stage of a greenhouse, where there is no drip, if the right temperature is kept up.   In Fig. 7 we show the plan we adopted with 9in.
pots : A, loam ; B, spawn ; C, mixture of manure and loam.   We
should mention that the same remarks as to keeping a latent
moisture in the whole mass apply to this plan as to all others.

CHAPTER XII.

CULTURE ON SHELVES.

THIS mode of cultivation is not so much used as formerly, and perhaps very rightly, but in restricted houses, where artificial heat can be applied, the saving of space effected by its use is very valuable. We, indeed, have had crops of mushrooms on these shelf beds quite equal to any on beds placed on the floor, but still the additional labour and trouble would be avoided where these latter beds were used. However, if one can get three beds in the space that otherwise only holds one, in small places the plan of shelf beds is worthy of adoption.

The material used for making the beds should contain rather more loam than that for beds on the floors, otherwise its preparation is practically the same, save that greater care should be taken that it is well prepared. The beds will need to be from 8in. to 10in in thickness, and must be well compressed, or the air will pass through them and cause rapid evaporation, making the whole too dry for the proper growth of the spawn.

Perhaps the sketch, shown at Fig. 8, of the house in which we had the greater success, will make our remarks more intelligible. The walls were 9in. thick, and a thatched roof covered the space within—about 8ft. wide. Two shelves, about 3ft. apart, were erected, and on these, and also on the floor, the beds were made, thus giving three beds where only one would otherwise have been placed. The house was originally built for another purpose, having a door at each end, and being heated by two 4in. pipes. The shelves were sparred with narrow pieces of wood about 3in. by 2in. square, and placed about an inch apart, and mushrooms were

produced almost as freely on the underside as on the surface of
the beds.

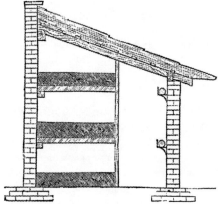

8.—House for Mushroom Culture on Shelves.

The way in which the beds were made is roughly shown in Fig. 9.

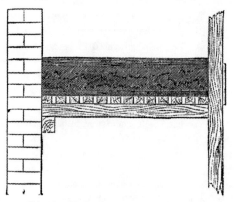

Fig. 9.—Mushroom Bed on a Shelf.

On the spars a layer of turfy loam, free from grass, and about an
inch thick, was placed; on this 7in. or 8in. of material prepared as

for ordinary beds, free from straw, and, after spawning, about 2in. of loam. The whole mass was kept well beaten together while the beds were being prepared, and the heat in the house was kept at from 65deg. to 67deg. A gentle dewing was given each day, to make up for evaporation, and in about seven weeks a good crop was the result, and the beds would keep bearing for about six or seven weeks. When the material appeared to be too dry a fair watering was given, which would not be needed till about the fifth week, and would last till the beds were done.

The chief points to be observed in this plan of culture are, the maintenance of the proper heat, which is a matter of much difficulty unless the house be suited to the work, and the keeping up of a proper amount of latent moisture in the beds, which latter point is best obtained by maintaining a moist but not saturated atmosphere. As a rule, it may be taken that more difficulty and care are needed with this method of culture than with almost all others, and practically the matter needs much more technical skill than is displayed by the average amateur gardener. Growing mushrooms on shelves is not the system that commends itself for the first attempt of an amateur, although he may and can be successful if he keeps up the right temperature and amount of latent moisture in the beds.

CHAPTER XIII.

CULTURE OUT OF DOORS.

WE have now reached a part of the subject that seems as little understood as is the growing of peaches or other choice fruit amongst amateurs, for while some dozens of men make a not inconsiderable income by growing for the London markets, few amateurs even achieve a moderate meed of success. Except in very hot weather, when the beds dry very quickly, outdoor work can be successfully kept up throughout the year, but in spring and autumn the least trouble is experienced, as a more equable amount of moisture exists in the atmosphere.

Autumn is, as a matter of fact, the best time for the culture of mushrooms out of doors, as then the beds last longest—the soil being charged with much heat, which it gives forth for some time, and, in fact, renders the surroundings of the beds very propitious for producing both heavy and lasting crops; to this warmth must be added the moisture of the air, which prevents undue evaporation and gives us in September, October, and November the best natural aids to production we can reasonably desire. Many market growers, who have open grounds exposed to all winds and weathers, combine spawn preparation with the culture of the mushroom, and on both they, as a rule, net good returns; but, on the other hand, others prefer sheltered spaces for the work. Personally, we like positions that are protected from the hottest rays of the sun, if it can possibly be managed in the dry months of June, July, and August, as the air dries up the beds quite fast enough without having the rays of the sun beating directly on the beds as well. We should, if possible, select a place under shady trees, or on the northern side of a high wall; but if such cool spots did not exist, we should do the best we could under the circumstances, and, by covering with additional litter, try to prevent the heat of the sun reaching the surface of the beds. In private places, where tidiness and neat appearance is a *sine quâ non*, this litter is not admissible, and the result is a failure in the crop of mushrooms, as might be expected.

In outdoor work it is as necessary to keep the beds sufficiently moist as when they are in houses, and unless enough litter is kept over them, they dry very quickly in very hot or windy weather; and, when once dry, it is a difficult matter to water them, owing to their ridge-like form. In cold weather enough covering must be put on to keep out the frost, for, while destroying the crop already produced, frost will kill the heat in the bed sufficiently to injure the active mycelium, and the result is the loss of the bed, which is a serious matter where manure is from 7s. to 10s. 6d. per load. The best litter is well-trodden stable straw which has been dried, and, to keep rain or snow off this, straw mats worked on hurdles, sacks, tarpaulins, or other additional coverings should be used, or, if the expense is not objected to, boarded covers, as used to cover unburnt bricks when drying on the hacks in a brickfield, are very good and durable; they, however, take two persons to move them about. Whatever is used, it is necessary meanwhile that it should fulfil the purpose intended, and not be of sufficient weight to press on the beds too heavily, or the mushrooms will come deformed. Too great heat will also produce badly-shaped mushrooms.

The materials should be prepared as before described, and when in a fit state should be made into long ridges about thirty inches wide at the base and three feet high. When making the beds, it is necessary to keep them well trodden and firm, as described for flat beds, and they should be patted over to make them flat on each side, otherwise the heat may escape too rapidly; and as the ridges are thrown up they should have some litter thrown over them to prevent too rapid evaporation, but at the same time too much should not be put on, or a sour fermentation will set in which will be fatal to the beds. When the heat has *declined* to 75deg. or 80deg., the beds should be spawned in the same manner as described for the other beds, and can be soiled down at once or left for as long a time as may be considered best in individual cases, but not less than 1½in. of soil should be applied. Of course, the covering should not be left off, because if such is done the wind will blow both heat and moisture out of the beds.

In six or seven weeks after the beds are spawned and covered with earth, the first gathering will be ready, and the litter should be carefully taken off, all mushrooms that are fit gathered, and the beds covered again at once, and from this date till the beds cease bearing they should be uncovered twice a week only. Should the soil get

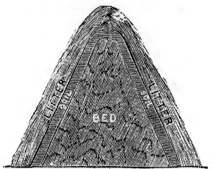

Fig. 10.—Sectional View of Ridge Bed.

dry, a sprinkling of water may be applied through a fine-rosed water can, but with care in covering this will not often occur. The beds last from six weeks to two months in bearing if properly covered and looked after, but, generally, it is a good system to make a fresh bed every fourth week if the materials can be readily obtained, as then a regular crop can be maintained, and seasons of scarcity will not occur. We do not, of course, refer to market work here, as, in that, a series of large crops at certain seasons pays better than a regular crop of medium weight all the year round; for when mushrooms are fetching a fair price then is the time they are most profitable to the market gardener. In Fig. 10

we give a sectional sketch of a bed, and in Fig. 11 a sketch of a straw covering we have found very useful for many purposes. It is 10ft. long, 4ft. wide, and the straw or sedge is about 2in. thick. The frame of slate batten is nailed together first, and then the straw is put on and laced down with tarred twine, and, if carefully done, will keep out rain and snow, and last for several years.

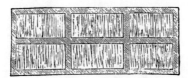

FIG. 11.—STRAW PROTECTING SCREEN.

Where there is a good roof, of course flat beds can be made, and these are, as a rule, most manageable to an amateur, and, in fact, it is not bad policy to make a boarded roof against a wall, where such exists, as good results are then almost certain, whereas with the ridges they are not so in the hands of amateurs.

CHAPTER XIV.

MUSHROOM ENEMIES.

THE most troublesome pests to the cultivator of mushrooms are woodlice, slugs, and snails, and sometimes mice and rats, for although these latter will not eat much (if any) of the crop, yet they will make nests and runs in the material of which the beds are composed, and cause much damage mechanically. There are also one or two flies and beetles which are injurious in the larval and perfect state, but not so much as to cause very serious damage to the crops, save in very exceptional cases, and for that reason we do not mention them here particularly.

Slugs may best be caught by placing small heaps of scalded bran or ordinary brewers' grains about the alleys between the beds, laying the heaps at night and cleaning them away with the slugs which are feeding on them in the morning.

Snails can only be got rid of by hand-picking, but they are (as are also slugs) fond of slices of wurtzel, turnips, &c., and if these are looked over about midnight the marauders can generally be caught. Perseverance is, however, very essential.

Woodlice are best kept down by cleanliness, but can be trapped by placing some cold boiled potatoes in small pots, covering with moss, and then placing in the haunts of the pests. These traps should be examined daily, and the woodlice turned into a bucket of hot water.

Rats and Mice should be trapped as soon as traces of them are discovered, or if this is not convenient they should be poisoned, because in a few months the progeny of one pair will be very large, and the damage they do proportionately increased.

Full recipes for the destruction of the majority of garden pests will be found in " Garden Pests and their Eradication," published by L. Upcott Gill, at 170, Strand, post free, 1s.

LaVergne, TN USA
28 September 2009
159248LV00001B/85/A